Tell Me So I Know

My Questions... Your Answers

Tell Me So I Know

My Questions... Your Answers

Paul Shike

Graceful Publishing
2015

First Printing: 2015

ISBN 978-0-9963441-1-1

Graceful Publishing
6723 Woodland Dr.
Dallas, TX 75225
www.tellmesoiknow.com
www.gracefulpublishing.com

Contents

Acknowledgments

Many thanks go out to my wonderful family, which instilled the desire for me to know more about their lives, memories and life lessons.

I appreciate the generous support from my friends, many of whom reserved copies of ***Tell Me So I Know*** in advance of it being published. I am certain you will feel rewarded for your investment as you engage with those special to you.

Thank you Jennifer Lassiter, for taking my work and refining it into a print-ready project. Finding a person with the talent to complete the layout and cover of this book was the final touch needed to make my dream of publishing this book come true.

I would like to thank Chandler Bjork. Chandler interpreted my vision for the cover to create the wonderful artwork for this book. I chose to use elephants for their association with having long memories. The image depicts the beliefs that they provide good luck with their raised trunks and display love by having their trunks wrapped. The outline of the "Tree of Life" is heart-shaped to symbolize the lifetime of love we share with the important people in our life.

Preface

I set out with the goal of creating a book to guide you through a number of questions to explore the life of someone special to you. This book also provides a place to record this information.

I hope you will use this book to engage with your parents, grandparents, aunts and uncles, children and other loved ones. Take the time to ask these questions to discover the favorites, life stories, beliefs and memories of those special to you. By sharing this process you will find the bond between each of you strengthened.

The two significant events that inspired me to create this book were the unexpected death of my father, Gene Shike, and witnessing the impact of Alzheimer's on my grandmother and aunt. It did not occur to me that the opportunity to ask them questions about their lives would suddenly end. I find myself wondering daily about the questions I wish I could have asked them. These unanswered questions leave a hollow space in my soul.

I received a call from my sister while I was traveling in Jacksonville, FL. She told me that my father was not feeling well and that the doctors had decided to admit him into the hospital. His kidneys had unexpectedly failed and the doctors said they did not think he had long to live. Shocked to hear this news, I immediately headed to Indiana. He passed eight hours after I first received the call.

Witnessing the impact of Alzheimer's on my grandmother and aunt inspired my writing as well. It seemed as if this horrible disease stole their memories overnight. It is difficult to experience the process of a loved one losing their ability to share their memories.

Many of my conversations with my father were about the latest sporting events. My conversations with my grandmother and aunt did not go much deeper than "how was your week?" I now understand how special it would have been to know their answers to questions such as "What was your favorite memory of me as a child?"

Embrace this book and use this process with the special people in your life. Seize the opportunity to gather this information first hand and strengthen the bonds that you share. Take questions from this book to learn at least one new thing about everyone you know.

It is easy to believe that "tomorrow" will be a good time to ask these questions. Many of the questions in this book I never thought of asking. Many of the questions I did not get around to asking. I certainly wish I knew my father's answers to the questions within this book. Please do not wait! Dad, I wish you could tell me so I know.

How to Begin

The greatest compliment that was ever paid me was when one asked me

what I thought, and attended to my answer.

~ Henry David Thoreau

Learning of the life experiences and special memories of an important person in your life will be an enriching process. The more we share and know about each other, the greater the opportunity to strengthen our relationships. Before beginning this journey with someone special, be sure to share with them why they are important to you.

The person you are interviewing will usually begin to answer the questions based on their understanding. Do not become bogged down by what exactly a question is asking. You will gain more by listening to the answers, than by debating the correct way to answer a question.

Respect that there are reasons for not wanting to share certain memories. There are no rules stating that the person must answer a question. Conversely, they may want to share their answers to some of the questions with only you. Honor all requests for confidentiality.

Be sure to respect the person's answers. In most cases, there is no right or wrong answer to a question. Avoid challenging them over the details of events. Challenges may lead to a breakdown in the discussion. Be positive and try to keep the discussion moving forward.

For each story, gather as many details as possible. Knowing that you went with your Grandpa Taylor to see the Brooklyn Dodgers vs. the New York Yankees provides a deeper understanding than the mere fact that you went to a baseball game with your grandpa. Details, such as names and places, will help to enhance and preserve the memories.

Be sure to ask "why" as the questions are answered. Discovering your parents' favorite song is great, but knowing why it is their favorite song will be better. Enjoy the additional questions that will certainly arise as you go through the book.

You may not always have the opportunity to sit down together and ask the questions. A great way to work through the book is to ask a few of the questions each time you talk over the phone. Consider scheduling a specific time each week to discuss a few of the questions. As you piece together the information over time, utilize this process to build a stronger relationship.

If you have siblings, consider a group discussion. You may get enhanced answers by asking these questions in a group. The dynamics of the group will help to enrich the discussion.

I do hope that you start sooner rather than later. You never know when you may lose the opportunity to discover this information. My advice is to begin today. Trust from my experience, once you cannot get the answers you will wish that you could go back in time to ask these questions.

Will You Tell Me So I Know?

These are the memories and life story of:

From interviews conducted by:

Date(s):

My relationship to this person is:

This person is special to me because:

Let's Get Started

An unexamined life is not worth living.

~ Socrates

This chapter is where the journey begins. You will start by discussing basic information such as your full name, birth date and place of birth. There are questions about early childhood and the things in life that you did not get to choose, such as your parents and siblings.

Be proud of your decision to embark upon this journey. Have fun, laugh, and cherish the memories. The first question is...

What is your full name?

Were you named after anyone? If so, why?

By what name do most people know you?

What other names have you used? Why?

Did you ever wish you were named or called something different?

What are your parents' names? When and where were they born?

What siblings do you have? When and where were they born?

What is the name of your spouse or significant other? When and where were they born?

When were you born? What is your current age?

Where were you born?

What stories do you know about your mother's pregnancy and your birth?

How much did you weigh when you were born?

What color was your hair as a child? Has it changed?

What color are your eyes?

What is your current height?

Have you ever wished you were taller or shorter?

How was your health as an infant?

What do you know about your baby items such as your blanket, stuffed animal, and/ or your first pair of shoes? Do you still have any of these items?

What stories do you know about you as an infant?

Do you have any tattoos? What is the story behind them?

Do you have any birthmarks, moles, scars, dimples or other distinguishing features?

How would you describe yourself today so someone could pick you out in a crowd?

Childhood

Even a minor event in the life of a child is an event of that child's world and thus a world event.

~ Gaston Bachelard

Childhood is an amazing time of one's life. As you recall a story, share your perception of the event from your view as a child. Answer the questions with as many details as you can remember. The details will help to improve the understanding of these memories.

What is you first childhood memory?

What is your favorite childhood memory?

How was your health as a child?

What were your thoughts as a child about your parents?

What were your favorite activities with your parents when you were a child?

What was your parent's favorite story to tell about something you said or did?

As a child, how did you get along with your siblings?

Who was your childhood best friend? Are you still friends?

What are some of the activities you did with your best friend?

What did you aspire to be when you grew up?

From your perspective as a child, what did you think about your house and neighborhood? How would you describe it now?

As a child, what are your memories of your pets?

What are some of your favorite birthday memories?

What toys do you remember having? Which one was your favorite?

Did you collect anything as a child? Do you still have any items from the collection?

What were some of your favorite childhood clothing items?

What were your favorite snack foods?

What was your favorite restaurant and food to order?

What was your favorite store to go to as a child? What about it do you remember?

What do remember about your first radio, TV, and record player?

What were your favorite TV shows and cartoons?

What is the first movie you remember watching?

What was your favorite song as a child?

What is the first book you remember reading?

What was your favorite book and why?

Where did you attend elementary and junior high school?

What is your first memory of going to school?

Who were your favorite teachers and why?

What memories do you have about how you got to and from school?

Were you ever in a play? What was it and what was your role?

What activities and sports did you participate in as a child?

What awards did you win as a child?

What do you remember about learning to ride a bike?

What is the first trip or vacation you remember?

What was your most memorable childhood adventure?

What is the most trouble you got into as a child?

What was the most dangerous thing you did as a child?

What was your worst injury as a child?

What weather events do you remember as a child?

What are your memories of major historic events?

What was the most memorable event you attended as a child?

What else would you like to share about your childhood?

High School and College

Live as if you were to die tomorrow. Learn as if you were to live forever.

~ Mahatma Gandhi

High school and college are a time in which you become much more independent. You start developing opinions, making decisions, and doing things on your own. Most of us started to drive, experienced our first dates, and established our best friends during this time.

Share the stories of the events that shaped your future. You may have had the best time of your life in high school or college. You may have struggled during this time. The questions in this chapter will help you to explore and share the stories behind these feelings.

Where did you go to high school?

What was your high school mascot?

How many students were in your graduating class?

How would you describe your high school experience?

Did you ever want to go to a different school? Why?

What were your rivals' stereotypes about your school?

Who were your best friends in high school?

How would you describe your peer group?

When not in school, where did you and your friends hang out?

Who from high school do you still consider to be close friends?

Who was the classmate that you most admired? Why?

Who was your nemesis and why?

Did you ever get into a fight? With whom and why?

Is anyone you went to school with famous? If so, how did they gain their fame?

What was your favorite subject and why?

What was your least favorite class and why?

How were your grades?

Who was your favorite teacher and why?

Who were the most influential people in your life during your high school years?

What did you think of your parents while you were in high school?

Did you participate in any sports? If so, what positions did you play and how well did you do?

Were you a cheerleader, on the drill team or in the band?

Did you play an instrument? Do you still play it?

Did you win any special awards?

What are your memories of your school dances?

What songs do you associate with your high school days?

Did you have a car in high school?

Who had the coolest car in school?

What was your dream car in high school?

What did you like to do when you were not at school?

What were your favorite summer activities?

Did you work? If so, what jobs did you have?

Did you babysit? Do you still see that person today?

Do you remember an event you felt was a crisis that you can laugh about now?

What was the most traumatic event you experienced while in high school?

What did you wish you could change about yourself during high school?

Looking back, what two things would you have done differently?

What was the best thing that happened to you while you were in high school?

Did you go to college or trade school? Where did you go and why?

What do you remember about your first day on campus?

What was your major when you started and why did you choose it?

Did you change your major during college? If so, why?

Who was the most influential person in the selection of your major and why?

What was your favorite class?

Who was your most memorable teacher? Why?

How were your grades?

Where did you live during your college days?

Were you in a fraternity or sorority? Which one? What was its reputation?

Did you participate in any college sports? What was your role?

In which non-academic activities did you participate?

What jobs did you have during college?

Were you a fan of your college sports teams? What events stand out in your mind?

Did your sports teams win any championships? What do you remember about them?

Who were your best friends in college? Who do you still talk with and see?

Where was your favorite place to go with your friends? Is it still there?

Who was your favorite local band? When was the last time you saw them?

What songs take you back to your college days?

Who from college do you want to know “what happened to them?”

What are your most memorable college experiences?

What story about your college days do you tell most frequently?

How would you describe your overall college experience?

What are your feelings when you return to the campus of your alma mater?

What do you think about the current status of your college?

Did you go to graduate school? If so, what degrees did you receive?

How do you feel your education prepared you for your career?

If you could go back in time, would you have taken different classes?

What advice would you give to someone starting college today?

Love and Marriage

Once in awhile, right in the middle of an ordinary life, love gives us a fairy tale.

~ Unknown Author

Relationships play a special role in our lives. This chapter covers an area where emotions run the deepest for most people. There are many lessons to learn from the sharing of stories about relationships, love and marriage.

While reminiscing and discussing the questions from this chapter, be sure to look for the twinkle in an eye or the appearance of a smile.

With whom did you have your first crush and why were you attracted to them?

____

____

____

____

____

With whom was your first kiss and what do you remember about it?

____

____

____

____

____

____

What do you remember about your first date?

____

____

____

____

____

____

When was the first time you told someone you loved them?

Whom do you consider your first true love? What was special about them?

Based on your life experiences, how would you now describe those feelings of love?

Do you currently know anything about this person?

Who was your worst heartbreak? What happened?

When and where did you meet your spouse?

What do you remember about the first time you met your spouse?

What qualities about this person attracted you to them?

When did you know it was love?

When and where did you get engaged?

What did your parents think about your engagement?

How long did you know each other before getting married?

When did you get married? How old were you and your spouse?

Where did you get married?

Who was in your wedding?

How many people attended your wedding? Did anyone show up unexpectedly?

What are your favorite memories of your wedding day?

Was there any drama on your wedding day?

What are your memories of your wedding reception?

What memories do you have of your Honeymoon? Where did you go?

Do you have any keepsakes from your wedding?

What was your most memorable wedding gift?

Which of your wedding gifts do you still have?

What special memories do you have about any of your anniversaries?

What is your most romantic memory?

What is the most memorable gift you have received from your spouse?

What have been your favorite things to do as a couple?

As a couple, what is "your song"? What memories does it bring back?

What is the most memorable trip or vacation you have taken together?

What is your favorite photo of your love?

What do you feel are the two most important factors for a successful relationship?

Whose relationship do you view as the standard for love? Why?

What is your advice about love?

All in the Family

A man travels the world over in search of what he needs, and returns home to find it.

~ George Moore

There is a special bond between the members of a family. Throughout life this bond is the source of many stories and memories. Grandparents, parents, and siblings are blessings in our life. They provide a level of comfort where the only explanation is "we are family."

In many cases, you are the sole person who knows a special story about a family member. By sharing your stories, you provide the opportunity to pass this information on to future generations.

Who do you know from each of the preceding generations of your family?

Great grandparents?

Grandparents?

Do you have any children? What are their names and ages?

What is your favorite memory of each of your children?

What is your favorite memory of your parents?

What is your favorite story about your spouse or significant other?

What is your favorite story about a sibling?

What is your favorite memory of each of your grandparents?

How would you describe the impact that your family has had in your life?

Who would you consider your favorite relative and why?

Who is the most famous member of your family?

What is your favorite story from a family function?

Which of your family traditions are the most important to you?

What are your most cherished family heirlooms and why?

What story would you most like to be passed on to future generations?

Faith

The great act of faith is when a man decides that he is not God.

~ Oliver Wendell Holmes, Jr.

There are different faiths and beliefs. We draw from the power of those beliefs, no matter which faith we choose. Use this chapter to discover the role that faith plays in the life of the person being interviewed.

Listen to the answers and encourage the sharing of these beliefs. Do not make judgments or try to impose your own beliefs on each other during this process. You may decide to use what you share during this chapter as the foundation for in-depth discussions in the future.

How would you describe your beliefs?

When do you remember faith first being introduced into your life?

What person has had the most influence on your spiritual life?

During what events in your life have you called upon your faith to help you?

Have your beliefs ever caused any problems in your life?

Have you ever questioned your faith? Why?

What are the most important benefits you feel your beliefs have had in your life?

What do you think others should know about your beliefs?

What is your advice about faith and a spiritual life?

The Working Life

Choose a job you love, and you will never have to work a day in your life.

~ Confucius

For many, the events in this chapter will span the most years of your life. Note how your perception of your jobs has changed over time. You may think your first job was the most difficult job in the world. Now, you may wish that your life were so simple.

The path you have taken has brought many people into your life. There are co-workers who inspired you, while you have inspired others. There are colleagues you have admired, and possibly someone who broke your spirit. All of these people impacted your life and who you are as a person.

Be proud of what you have accomplished. Use your experiences and what you have learned as a reference point for providing and sharing your career advice.

What was your first job?

How did you find your first job?

What jobs have you had during your life?

What has been your favorite job?

Which job did you most dislike?

What job did you want, but did not get?

Which job do you feel provided the most learning experiences?

What is your dream job?

Who was your favorite and least favorite boss?

What person do you feel had the most influence on your career path?

Which co-worker do you feel was the most influential in your career?

Who is the person that you feel you most impacted during your career?

Who is your best friend from work?

What rewards and recognition have you received as a result of your work?

What do you feel is your greatest career accomplishment?

What do you consider the most disappointing event in your career?

What is your advice on balancing your work and home life?

What advice would you give to someone beginning their career?

Money

Too many people spend money they earned...to buy things they don't want...to impress people that they don't like.

~ Will Rogers

Throughout your life money (or the lack of it) has had a direct impact on the decisions you have made, what you have purchased, and what you have experienced. The following questions explore these memories from childhood through the present. Share the advice and insight you have derived from these first-hand experiences.

As a child, what was your perception of your family's financial situation?

Looking back as an adult, how would you now describe your family's financial situation as it was when you were a child?

During your childhood, were there any significant changes in your family's financial situation?

When you were young, where did you keep the money you saved?

What items do you remember buying as a child?

What was your most expensive purchase as a child?

What do you remember about opening your first bank account?

What is the purchase for which you felt the most excited?

What is your most extravagant purchase?

What item that you purchased in the past do you wish you still had?

What purchase do you feel was your greatest waste of money?

What is the most money you have received as a gift? From whom did you receive it?

What is the first work for which you remember getting paid?

How much money did you make in your first job?

Which paycheck are you most proud of?

What was your best investment?

What was your worst investment?

What was your most significant financial crisis?

What would you do differently in regards to managing your money?

What is the largest amount of cash you have had in your possession and why?

What is the largest amount of money you have lost? How did you lose it?

Have you ever been robbed? What happened?

Who in your life has given you the best financial advice? What was it?

How has your financial situation changed during your life?

What is your advice regarding money and finances?

Holidays and Vacations

No man needs a vacation so much as the man who has just had one.

~ Elbert Hubbard

Holidays and vacations are a time to escape from the pressures of everyday life. These are times typically shared with the special people in our life. For many, some of their best memories have been made during holidays and vacations.

Take this opportunity to reminisce and share the special moments and memories from your holidays and vacations.

What is your favorite holiday and why?

What are your first memories of the holidays?

What are your fondest holiday memories as a child?

What are you favorite holiday memories as an adult?

What is the most memorable gift you have received?

What is something you wished for, but never received?

What is the most memorable gift you have given to someone?

What is your favorite holiday picture?

What are your favorite holiday foods and snacks?

What is your favorite holiday outfit?

What special holiday traditions do you remember?

What traditions do you want to be carried on by your family?

What was the first Halloween costume you remember? Which one was your favorite?

What is the first vacation that you can recall ever taking?

What was your favorite vacation?

What is your favorite memory from a vacation?

Where was your favorite vacation picture taken? Who is in it?

Are your vacations spur of the moment or well planned?

What is your best advice on how to pack for a vacation?

Do you have a favorite place where you have vacationed more than once?

Which vacation destination do you want to visit again?

Where would you like to vacation that you haven't been before?

What are your favorite activities while on vacation?

What is the most majestic site you have seen while traveling?

What is the most memorable food you have eaten while on vacation?

What is the most unusual thing to happen to you while on vacation?

Who have you unexpectedly run into while on vacation?

What is your worst experience while on vacation?

What are the states and countries you have visited?

What souvenirs have you acquired while on vacation?

What injuries have you or someone else experienced while vacationing?

Cars and Transportation

Any customer can have a car painted any colour that he wants so long as it is black.

~ Henry Ford

Cars and transportation are now a large part of most people's lives. Many people are very passionate about the cars they have owned. Share the memories of your parents' cars, your first car and your favorite car.

If you have traveled by air, share your memories of your first experience on an airplane. Think about your experiences with unusual modes of transportation. For some, the use of a horse-drawn wagon has been a part of their everyday life. Enjoy recalling and sharing these memories as you discuss the questions in this chapter.

What are your first memories about cars?

What cars did your family have while you were growing up?

Which family car was your favorite?

What is your favorite color of car?

What was your first car and what did it cost?

What were the makes and models of all the cars you have owned?

Of the cars that you owned, which was your favorite?

Of the cars that you owned, which one did you like least?

What was the most expensive car you have ever purchased?

What was the least expensive car you have ever purchased?

Did you make changes to any of your cars?

Which of your previous cars do you wish you still owned?

What is your dream car?

What are your memories of driving your first motorized vehicle?

How did you learn to drive a car?

When did you get your driver's license?

Why were you given your first ticket?

What are your memories of other tickets you've received? What are the stories behind them?

What is the fastest you have driven a car?

Have you been involved in any serious accidents?

What memories do you have of your longest trip by car?

What are your memories of your friends' cars?

Have you ever owned a motorcycle? If so, what kind?

What do you remember about your first experience flying on a plane?

Is there an event that frightened you while traveling on an aircraft?

Have you ever traveled by private plane?

Have you ever flown in a helicopter?

Have you ever piloted (or wished that you had piloted) a plane, helicopter or hot air balloon?

What is the furthest you have walked or hiked?

What is the furthest you have ridden a bike?

What are your experiences utilizing animals for transportation?

What is your most memorable experience involving animal powered transportation?

How has transportation evolved during your lifetime?

Tell Me Your Favorite

A human being has a natural desire to have more of a good thing than he needs.

~ Mark Twain

We all have our favorites. In this chapter you will share one hundred of your favorite items. Answer the questions as quickly as possible. The first answer that pops into your head is most often your favorite.

Breakfast Food ______________________________

Doughnut ______________________________

Cereal ______________________________

Jelly/Jam ______________________________

Bread ______________________________

Sandwich ______________________________

Cheese ______________________________

Fruit ______________________________

Vegetable ______________________________

Cut of Meat ______________________________

Fish ______________________________

Pizza ______________________________

Salad Dressing ______________________________

Spice ______________________________

Dessert ______________________________

Ice Cream ______________________________

Girl Scout Cookie ______________________________

Cake ______________________________

Perfect Meal ______________________________

Candy ______________________________

Gum ____

Road Trip Snack ____

Soft Drink ____

Coffee ____

Beer ____

Wine ____

Hard Liquor ____

Mixed Drink ____

Fast Food Restaurant ____

Frequently Visited Restaurant ____

Special Occasion Restaurant ____

Color ____

Smell ____

Flower ____

Tree ____

Store ____

Brand You are Most Loyal ____

Piece of Furniture ____

Kitchen Utensil ____

Appliance ____

Tool ______________________________

Car ______________________________

House ______________________________

City Lived In ______________________________

School ______________________________

Location Visited ______________________________

City Visited ______________________________

Theme Park ______________________________

Beach ______________________________

Lake ______________________________

Park ______________________________

Monument ______________________________

Museum ______________________________

Souvenir ______________________________

Keepsake ______________________________

Collectible ______________________________

Time of Day ______________________________

Day of the Week ______________________________

Weather/Temperature ______________________________

Season ______________________________

Holiday ______________________________

Sport to Play ______________________________

Exercise ______________________________

Board Game ______________________________

Card Game ______________________________

Outdoor Activity ______________________________

Way to Relax ______________________________

Singer ______________________________

Band ______________________________

Concert Attended ______________________________

Song ______________________________

Holiday Song ______________________________

Instrument ______________________________

Actor ______________________________

Actress ______________________________

Comedian ______________________________

Cartoon Character ______________________________

News Anchor ______________________________

President ______________________________

Movie ______________________________

TV Show ______________________________

Magazine ______________________________

Book ______________________________

Fairytale ______________________________

Broadway Play ______________________________

Sports Star ______________________________

Sports Team ______________________________

Sport to Watch ______________________________

Outfit ______________________________

Blue Jeans ______________________________

Shoes ______________________________

Pajamas ______________________________

Clothing Brand ______________________________

Piece of Jewelry ______________________________

Perfume/Cologne ______________________________

Picture of Yourself ______________________________

Vacation Picture ______________________________

Family Picture ______________________________

Pet ______________________________

Exotic Animal ______________________________

What are three of your least favorite things?

What three things make you the happiest?

154 Choices

Sometimes making a choice has no right or wrong answer or negative outcome. We simply get to choose between two good things.

~Paul Shike

This chapter has a list of 154 pairs of items. Ask the person you are interviewing to select the item in each pair that is their favorite or best describes them.

To add a fun twist, go through the list and pick the answer you believe the person you are interviewing will select before asking the questions. Do not show the person you are interviewing your selections until after they have made their choices. To keep track of both answers, underline your pick and circle their choice.

Compare how each of you answered the questions. Use the three questions at the end of the chapter to aid your discussion.

Bacon or Sausage

Fried Eggs or Scrambled

Pancakes or Waffles

Toast or Biscuit

White Bread or Wheat Bread

French Fries or Onion Rings

Hamburger or Hot Dog

Ketchup or Mustard

Soup or Salad

Pizza or Spaghetti

Marinara or Alfredo

Cheese Pizza or Supreme

Baked or Fried

Steak or Chicken

Turkey or Ham

Grilled or Sushi

Fresh or Frozen

Sweet or Sour

Spicy or Mild

Sugar or Sweet'N Low®

Apple or Orange

Pie or Cake

Ice Cream Cone or Bowl

Popsicle® or Fudgsicle®

Nuts or Berries

Gum or Mints

Lays® or Pringles®

Cheetos® or Doritos®

Popcorn or Peanuts

Milk Chocolate or Dark Chocolate

Snickers® or Reese's®

Almond Joy® or Mounds®

Cotton Candy or Funnel Cake

Coffee or Tea

Pepsi® or Coke®

Beer or Wine

Can or Bottle

Breakfast or Dinner

Buffet or Table Service

Paper Plates or China

Wash or Dry the Dishes

Cook or Clean

Bath or Shower

Pool or Hot Tub

Inside or Outside

Sun or Shade

Spring or Fall

City or Country

Beach or Mountains

Camp or Hotel

Destination or Journey

Highway or Scenic Route

Sandcastle or Snowman

Fireplace or Campfire

Sink or Swim

Hare or Tortoise

Lover or Fighter

Captain or Mate

Calm or Crazy

Give or Receive

Pitch or Hit

Organized or Messy

Lead or Follow

Patient or Impatient

Focused or ADD

Early or Late

Walk or Run

Stand or Dance

Sit or Pace

Whisper or Scream

Morning or Night

Work or Play

Appointment or Walk-in

Teach or Learn

Draft or Edit

Prepared or Wing It

Smell The Roses or Rush

The Kite or The String

King or Jester

File or Pile

Talk or Listen

Quiet or Loud

Remember or Forget

Hawk or Chicken

Audio or Visual

Diamond or Emerald

Old and Wise or Young and Crazy

Call or Text

Fire or Ice

Love or War

Tough or Meek

Explode or Implode

Create or Destroy

Graceful or Klutz

Rebel or Conform

Bend or Break

Sugarcoat or Blunt

Get Mad or Get Even

Rebuild or Move On

Republican or Democrat

Truth or Dare

Ask For Directions or Get Lost

Salary or Commission

In The Box or Out Of The Box

Future or Past

Hot or Cold

Change or Status Quo

Repair or Replace

Do It Yourself or Hire

Share or Possessive

New or Used

Shop or Buy

Spend or Save

Cash or Credit

Collect or Dispose

Crosswalk or Jaywalk

Window or Isle

Crowds or Solace

Rock or Country

Jazz or Classical

Elvis or The Beatles

Sing or Hum

Guitar or Piano

Waltz or Jitterbug

Slots or Card Games

Football or Basketball

Golf or Miniature Golf

Circus or Fair

Movie or Book

Comedy or Drama

Soap Opera or Game Show

Newspaper or Magazine

Cinderella or Snow White

Mickey or Goofy

Windows® or Mac®

Cat or Dog

Drive or Passenger

Car or Truck

Convertible or Hardtop

Two Door or Four Door

Harley or Honda

Drive or Fly

Glasses or Contacts

Preppy or Grunge

Pants or Shorts

Shoes or Boots

Sweater or Sweatshirt

Sandals or Barefoot

Laces or Loafers

Silver or Gold

Sofa or Recliner

Modern or Antique

Paint or Stain

Carpet or Hardwood Floors

How many of the questions did you answer the same?

Did you think that this number would be higher or lower?

Which answers most surprised you?

I Wish Someone Would Have Told Me

The best time to plant a tree was twenty years ago. The second best time is now.

~ Chinese Proverb

Hindsight is said to be twenty-twenty. There are times you say, "I wish someone would have told me." It is not unusual to feel that with more knowledge, events would have been handled differently or have turned out differently. Use the advice from someone special to avoid the "I wish someone would have told me" moments in the future.

What do you wish someone would have told you about the opposite sex?

What do you wish someone would have told you about dating?

What do you wish someone would have told you about love?

What do you wish someone would have told you about marriage?

What do you wish someone would have told you about in-laws?

What do you wish someone would have told you about children?

What do you wish someone would have told you about siblings?

What do you wish someone would have told you about dealing with idiots?

What do you wish someone would have told you about managing your time?

What do you wish someone would have told you about manners?

What do you wish someone would have told you about school?

What do you wish someone would have told you about work?

What do you wish someone would have told you about money?

What do you wish someone would have told you about cars?

What do you wish someone would have told you about holidays?

What do you wish someone would have told you about your health?

What do you wish someone would have told you about cooking?

What do you wish someone would have told you about life?

Did I Tell You the Story?

It's not the years in your life that count. It's the life in your years.

~ Abraham Lincoln

We all have stories we love to tell others. Think about the stories that bring back smiles and great memories. There are both firsthand stories from our experiences and stories shared by family members and friends. Recall the stories that you have shared multiple times during your life.

Document what you learn about these stories. Over time, it may become difficult to recall these details from your memory.

What is your favorite story about your childhood?

What is your favorite story about you?

What is your favorite story that you most often tell others?

What is the story you tell that gets the most laughs?

What is a story you remember telling at your high school reunion?

What is your favorite story about the person interviewing you?

What was your closest brush with death?

What is your favorite vacation story?

What is your favorite story about you winning something?

What is your favorite story about a friend?

What is your favorite story about an event you attended?

What is the story behind you learning one of life's lessons?

The Future and the Past

Life is divided into three terms -that which was, which is, and which will be. Let us learn from the past to profit by the present, and from the present to live better in the future.

~ William Wordsworth

Life has a past, present and future. How different would your life be if you could go back and change the past or see into the future? Who from your past do you wish you could spend one more day with? If this were possible, what would you want to do with them?

Use this opportunity to explore your past and your thoughts about the future.

What is one thing that you hope to achieve that you have not yet accomplished?

If you could see into the future, what would you want to know?

If you could see into the future, what would you not want to know?

What are two things you would like to happen in the future?

What are your thoughts on what the future has in store for you?

What is the decision you most regret making during your lifetime?

If you could change your past, what are two things that you would do differently?

How would these changes impact your life?

What was the best day of your life?

Who would you like to meet during your lifetime?

Who have you not forgiven for something they have done? Do you wish you had?

How do you want to be remembered?

If you could bring two people back and spend a day with them, who would they be? What would you do with them?

For what five things are you the most grateful?

1.

2. ______________________________

____

____

____

____

3. ______________________________

____

____

____

____

4. ______________________________

____

____

____

____

5. ______________________________

____

____

____

____

Technology and Science

It is strange that only extraordinary men make the discoveries, which later appear so easy and simple.

~Georg C. Lichtenberg

Think of the things that have changed during your life. The list may include items such as automobiles, electricity in the home, indoor plumbing, radios, telephones, color TV, laptop computers and/or recent developments like the iPhone.

Explore the stories associated with the most memorable changes in technology and science you have experienced. Enjoy recalling your feelings and reactions the first time you were introduced to a new technology.

We have learned throughout life that the only constant in the world is change.

As a child, what were the new technology items you remember your family acquiring?

What were the most memorable technological and scientific discoveries you remember as a child?

Which technology items do you feel have most significantly impacted your life?

Which technology items do you feel have had the most impact on the world?

What is one technology item you purchased that you felt was a waste of money?

What are two technology items you have wanted, but never acquired?

What do you feel have been the most memorable medical innovations during your lifetime?

What advancements in medical technology have been critical in helping you or someone close to you?

Service to our Country

The nation which forgets its defenders will be itself forgotten.

~ Calvin Coolidge

Service to our country is a noble act and an important chapter in a person's life. There are those that volunteer and others that have been drafted to serve our country. We need to recognize these brave men and women as heroes.

Experiences vary from serving our country, and each person's life may have been affected differently. There are those that incurred life-changing injuries. Some may not want to discuss the horrors they experienced. For many, this is the most rewarding time of their life.

There are those who make a career of serving their country. Others see it as a brief stop along the road of life.

Use this chapter to learn about the hero within the person with whom you are sharing this process.

Who was the inspiration for your decision to join the military?

How long did you serve?

What is the highest rank you achieved?

In which branch did you serve?

Why did you select the branch in which you served?

To which division, wing, ship or specialty group where you assigned?

What is the history of this group? What is their motto?

What are your memories of boot camp or basic training?

What were the specialized trainings and/or schools you attended?

Which training was the most difficult?

Which training was the one you enjoyed the most?

Where have you been stationed?

On your deployments, where were you sent and how long were you deployed?

What do you remember about your deployments?

What medals and accommodations have you received?

With whom from your military career do you continue to stay in contact?

What experiences from the military do you still apply to your everyday life?

What is your advice about joining the military?

One Last Question

What question should I ask that I didn't?

65396116R00107

Made in the USA
Charleston, SC
23 December 2016